Stuckey's Venison Recipes

First Timers to Seasoned Chiefs

Stuckey's Venison Recipes

First Timers to Seasoned Chiefs

By
Mike J. Stuckey Sr.
&
Michael J. Stuckey Jr.

"Stuckey Publishing 2016"

SHORT NOTE

There is a feeling of self achievement and satisfaction about catching 'n' cooking big game. If the day would ever come that we were solely dependent upon our own resources in order to survive, I believe we would get along handsomely. For this reason, one has to learn the cooking capability of wild meat. For starters, there are a few exceptions: wild meat does not contain fat. One would have to acquire a supply of fat for cooking. Secondly, big game animals run wild, resulting in their steaks and roasts being a dry and/or stringy meat. When provisions are not made to address these deficiencies. Much of the exceptions depend on proper field dressing and the cooling of the deer afterwards. This is the beginning of the responsibilities of the Hunter.

Once you reach home with your big game, you're onto a whole other set of problems. You have to hang, skin, and butcher the deer in freezing temperatures. This consists of occasionally aging, but always cutting, wrapping, labeling, and freezing each package so it can be later conveniently handled in the kitchen for cooking. If you are not a butcher or have no experience in this technique, you do have other options. You can find a butcher, possibly from your local food store, if you are acquainted with him, or possibly a friend who is also a hunter. No matter whether you or somebody else attends to this matter, the deer should be stored or kept in freezing temperatures while butchering in order to preserve that meat. The portions that you cut up and package or that your butcher packages should be wrapped tightly, eliminating air pockets and moisture. Saran wrap, commonly used 'n' known as plastic wrap, works good for the purpose because it is moisture and vapor resistant. Each package should be broken down into sizes designed for cooking all at one time. (do not re-wrap and freeze after meat is thawed. This will cause it to spoil). A trick would be to include a sheet of waxed paper between any individual steaks, chops, fillets, etc. that are in the same package. This allows for easy separating at a later time. Each package of wrapped meat should be frozen as quickly as possible, preferably in below zero temperatures at first, and then later on moved into your standard freezer. Depending on your selected dish, the frozen game can be thawed or un-thawed. Keep in mind, any meat that is not thawed requires additional cooking time. This additional time will depend on the shape and size of the cut.

If cooking frozen meat, use a lower cooking temperature to prevent the meat from drying out. For this reason, I would suggest thawing the meat first.

Due to the fact that most big game has a general leanness, it keeps especially well. I would recommend, to have the most exquisite flavor, texture and to relish in each mouthful, you should eat it before the next hunting season. If by chance, your big game is a bear, the meat should be used within four months, to be at its richest and tastiest point. Items such as a heart, liver, kidneys and tongue will only keep for three months at 0°. Keep in mind local laws determine both the storage and limitations of possession of big-game. Once you've decided to cook big game meat, you're onto a whole other set of problems and that is where this recipe book comes in. The Venison in each and every recipe, can be change to suit the big game meat of your choice.

Mike J. Stuckey Sr.
Michael J. Stuckey Jr.

Michael J. Stuckey Jr. 1986

Mike J. Stuckey Sr. 1971

Pride & Honor

A.S.N.F. 2-24-13

Never Goodby:

Thank you, Dad for listening, caring and defending, for supporting, being gentle, vigilant 'n' protective. For giving and sharing all the many things you've done, all the times that you were there, you've been a rock to lean against in times of stress and strife. You may have thought I didn't see, or that I didn't hear, all of the life lessons you taught me. But I got every word. You built a strong foundation, no one can take away. You gave me honor, morals, pride, dignity, standards, respect of ones self and for others. To stand behind doing what is rite, even if it is illegal or morally wrong!! To hunt, field dress, skin and butcher, to cook. All of thees thing I've learned, taught by my Father and his before him, as I will to mine!!

Though I might not say it, I appreciate all you've done. I've grown up with your values, and I'm very glad I did. Without you, Dad, I wouldn't be The man I've become today. So richly blessed is how I feel, For having you as my father, so here's to you, my best friend, my dad..... I will see you again, at the end of this life or in the next.

Recipe Index

CONTENTS

Short Note

Dedication

1 Sauce

Venison basting sauce   2

2 Marinated Venison

Venison marinade   4

Marinated Venison   5

Marinated Venison steak   6

Burgundy steak's or chops   7

Saddle of Venison   8

Venison Ribs   9

Marinated Meat on a Stick 1   10

3   Steak's

Venison steak 1   12

Venison steak 2   13

Smothered venison steak   14

Pepper Steak   15

Skillet Fried Steak   16

Venison and Burgundy   17

Venison steak 3   18

Mandarin Venison   19

Venison Scallopini   20

Venison Steak Piquant   21

Venison chow Mein   22

Venison Ragout   23

4   Swiss Steak

Venison Swiss steak 1   26

Venison Swiss steak 2   28

Venison Swiss steak 3   29

Venison Swiss steak 4   30

Venison Swiss steak 5   31

Stuffed Slices Venison   32

5   Chops

Barbecued Venison Chops with   34
Savory Butter

Venison Chops Parmesan   35

Venison Chops   36

Broiled Venison Chops   37

6 Cutlets

Venison Cutlets   40

Venison Cutlets 1   41

Venison Cutlets 2   42

Texas Fried Venison   43

French Fried Venison   44

Venison Sticks   45

7 Roast

Venison Pot Roast   48

Venison Pot Roast with   49
Vegetables

Venison Roast   50

Venison Shanks with Rosemary   51

8 Stew

Venison Stew with White Wine 54

Venison Stew 1 56

Venison Stew 2 57

Venison Stew 3 58

Venison Stew 4 60

Hunter's Stew 61

Fancy Venison Stew 63

Venison Crock-pot Stew 64

9 Chop-meat

Ground Venison 66

Deer Burgers 67

Venison Burgers 68

Venison Meatballs 69

Venison Meatballs 2 70

Hunter's Chili 71

Texas Venison Chili 72

Grandma's Venison Chilli 73

Venison Meatloaf 74

10   Oven

Dutch Oven Venison	76
Venison with Sour Cream	77
Oven Venison	78
Rice for above dish	79
Venison Loaf	80
Venison Meat Loaf	81
Smothered Venison 1	82
Smothered Venison 2	83
Venison Ragout	84
Venison Ragout with Onions	85
North Woods Venison Casserole	87
Barbecued Venison Ribs	88
Luau Venison	89
Venison Stroganoff	90
Venison Roast	91
Sweet 'n' Sour Venison Tenderloin	92
Split Stuffed Pepper	93

11   Grilled

     Grilled Loin   96

     Spicy Barbecued Roast Venison   97

12   Innards & Specials

     Pickled Venison Heart   100

     Venison Heart   101

     Heart of Venison 2   102

     Fried Liver   103

     Venison Liver 1   104

     Venison Liver 2   105

     Deer Tongue   106

     Pit Cooked Venison   107

     Spiced Dried Venison   108

     Venison Mincemeat   109

     Venison Pot Pie   110

     Venison Sausage   111

     Deer Sausage   112

     Brine Cured Venison Roll   113

Venison Chips	114
Fried Deer Brain	115
Baked Deer Brain	116

Cooks Notes

Cooks Notes

1983

1
SAUCE

Venison basting sauce:

1 cup chicken bouillon
½ cup dried red wine
½ cup tomato sauce
2 tablespoons olive oil
2 tablespoons grated onion
1 garlic clove, peeled and minced
1 tablespoon salt
½ tablespoon crumbled dried rosemary
and/or chopped fresh rosemary
¼ tablespoon pepper
A pinch of cayenne pepper

Combine all ingredients in a small saucepan and heat to a boil. Reduce heat to a simmer, and keep sauce warm while basting your venison shanks.

2
MARINATED VENISON

Venison marinade

4 tablespoons olive oil
1 or 2 Fresh squeezed limes
½ glass Orange juice
1 glass of red wine
1 tablespoon salt
½ tablespoon freshly ground pepper
2 tablespoons curry
2 tablespoons ginger
2 tablespoons grated onion

Combine all ingredients thoroughly. Cut venison into 1 inch or 1 ½ inch pieces. Pour marinade over meat in a container or freezer bag. Marinate meat for at least 2 hours before cooking.

Marinated Venison

> 2 lemons, juiced
> or 1 lemon and ½ cup tarragon wine
> vinegar
> 2 onions, sliced
> 1 tablespoon chili powder
> ½ cup water
> 2 tablespoons salt
> 2 bay leaves
> ¼ tablespoon black pepper
> ½ cup Ketchup
> 1 garlic clove, minced

Combine all ingredients thoroughly. Pour over Venison in a covered container. Turn meat twice-daily. Total Marinate hours 48.

Marinated venison steaks

4 thick, venison steaks
1 onion, sliced
1 tablespoon salt
½ tablespoon white pepper
1 carrot, sliced
2 bay leaves
A pinch of thyme
A pinch of rosemary
2/3 cup dry white wine
8 tablespoons olive oil
2 tablespoons butter

Season venison steaks generously with salt and pepper. Combine onion, carrot, wine, 6 Tablespoons olive oil and seasonings in a large bowl. Marinate meat for one hour. Place remaining olive oil and butter in frying pan Saute marinated venison steaks on high heat for 3 minutes on each side

Burgundy stakes or chops

8 steaks or chops 1 ½ inch thick
1/3 cup butter
½ pound fresh mushrooms sliced
6 slices of bacon
¼ cup minced onion
½ cup diced celery
Freshly ground pepper
Seasoned all-purpose flour
Burgundy Wine

Place steaks in a shallow pan. Pour wine over steaks just shy of covering. Sprinkle excessively with pepper. Marinate overnight.

Next day. Remove meat from marinade and dry on paper towels. Save leftover marinade. Coat steaks or chops in seasoned flour. Sauté in butter until browned and tender. In a separate frying pan, set heat to simmer and add in 2 tablespoons butter, all the mushrooms, bacon, onion and celery. When ingredients are simmering add leftover wine marinade and bring to a boil. Place meat on a plate and pour the sauce, with vegetables, over the meat, then serve.

Saddle of venison

Lard Saddle of Venison Bacon
½ bottle Burgundy Wine
½ tsp. black pepper
2 white onions, sliced
1 cup celery & parsley leaves
1 tsp. salt
2 bay leaves, crushed
1 tsp. thyme
4 cloves
3 shallots
2 oz. butter

Place Lard saddle of Bacon in covered pot. Marinate 36 hours in all ingredients except shallots and butter. Turn often. Roast 40 minutes per lb at 450°F, basting often. Remove meat, and prepare gravy from marinade, adding shallots and butter. Add 1 tsp wine. Simmer 5 minutes.

Venison Ribs

In sauce pan, combine the following and bring to a boil:

> 1 cup chili sauce
> 1 ½ cups water
> ¼ cup steak sauce
> 2 tbsp. lemon juice
> ½ tsp. chili powder
> ½ tsp. salt

Marinate ribs for 48 hours in vinegar/water solution: (1 part vinegar, 3 parts water) with: 2 bay leaves, 2 tbsp. Salt, and 1 sliced onion. Refrigerate while marinating. Dry pieces and put in a shallow roasting pan. Brush Ribs with melted butter Roast at 450° for 30 minutes. Turn the oven temperature to 350°, then cover the meat with sauce. Bast liberally, coating with the above boiled sauce. Baste the meat at 15 minute intervals until the ribs are tender, 1 to 1 ½ more hours.

Marinated Meat on a Stick 1

2 lbs. venison round steak
¼ cup olive oil
¼ cup dry red wine
2 tbsp. Worcestershire
1 tsp. garlic salt
½ tsp. dried oregano
½ tsp. salt
¼ tsp. pepper

Remove fat and bone from meat and cut meat into 1" cubes. Mix remaining ingredients and pour over meat in a mixing bowl. Marinate for 2 hrs, stirring occasionally. Thread meat on individual skewers and broil, over charcoal or in the oven, turning to brown each side, about 3 minutes on each side.

3
STEAKS

Venison steak 1:

4 to 6 Deer steaks
1 large sliced onion
2 cloves garlic
½ cup, water
1 cup flour
1 tablespoon salt
1 tablespoon pepper
Vegetable oil

Season flour with salt and pepper.
Completely flour deer steaks. Add Vegetable
oil and floured deer steaks to iron skillet.
Brown, then flip and add onion garlic and
water. Cover and simmer 30 minutes.

Goes great over steamed rice

Venison steak 2:

    4 round steaks
    1 small onion, finely chopped
    1 cup flour
    2 tablespoon fat
    1 tablespoon salt
    1 teaspoon pepper

Cover steaks in onion. Roll steaks in flour. Place fat in large skillet, melt, then add steaks. Season with salt and pepper. Drizzle any remaining onion over top. Place steaks over high heat until brown, Turn to brown other side. Reduce temperature to a mild simmer. Add ½ cup boiling water and simmer for 30 min for younger deer, up to 1 hr for older deer. Add water as needed during simmering.

Smothered venison steak:

    4 Venison steaks or 2 rounds
    ½ teaspoon salt
    ½ teaspoon pepper
    A dash of garlic salt
    1 cup flour
    1 large onion, sliced
    12 peppercorns
    1 tablespoon Worcestershire sauce
    2 Tbsp. Oil

    In a freezer bag, add flour, salt, pepper and garlic salt. Cover steaks and surround with mix.

    Brown in oil. After browning add the last of ingredients with an additional 1 cup water. Reduce heat and simmer for 2 hours

Pepper Steak:

2 tablespoons crushed peppercorn
4 Loin Steaks, 1 inch thick
1 stick butter or margarine
1 cup beef broth
½ cup heavy cream
3 oz brandy

Thoroughly rub the 1 inch thick steaks with softened butter or margarine. Cover each side of the steaks with crushed peppercorns, one side at a time. With the side of the knife, press the seasoning into the meat. Let stand one hour at room temperature. Preheat your frying pan, melting ¼ stick butter in it. Sear each steak for one minute on each side. Remove steaks from skillet and keep warm.

Pour one cup of canned beef broth, heavy cream, and Brandy in pan and stir continuously over high heat for 3 minutes. Plate steaks and pour sauce over them.

This goes well with mashed potatoes

Skillet Fried Steak

2 Venison round steaks, pounded
¾ cup all-purpose flour
¼ tablespoon garlic salt
1 tablespoon salt
¼ tablespoon pepper
1 Vegetable Oil
1 beef bouillon cube
1 cup water
1 tablespoon Bottled brown bouquet
   sauce
Dash of Worcestershire sauce

Cut steaks into serving size pieces. Combine about ½ cup flour, garlic salt, salt and pepper Mix thoroughly. cover steaks with mix and pound into steak. Pour 1 cap of oil into hot skillet, brown both sides of each steak and remove Venison from skillet. Drain skillet, keeping 3 to 4 tablespoons of the fry oil. Return skillet to heat and add the 3 to 4 tablespoons of fry oil back to skillet. Dissolve bouillon cube in 1 cup water, set aside. Slowly stir ¼ cup flour into oil in frying pan. Slowly add dissolved bouillon cube, Worcestershire sauce, and bouquet sauce. Stir until thickened. Place Venison back into skillet, cover. Simmer over low heat for 30 minutes.

Venison and burgundy

4 – 1 inch thick venison steaks.
1 teaspoon salt
¼ teaspoon freshly ground black
pepper
1/8 teaspoon parsley flakes
½ stick butter
2 ½ cup Burgundy wine
1 can golden mushroom soup
Rosemary

Warm Steaks to room temperature,
sprinkle both sides with salt, black pepper and
parsley flakes. Rub liberally with rosemary.
Add butter to frying pan and brown both sides
of steaks. Add Burgundy wine, and bring to a
slow boil. Cover and simmer over low heat for
1 ½ hours or until tender. Check periodically.
If steaks look like they are becoming dry, add
more wine. When Venison is done, remove and
place on a platter. Quickly mix the mushroom
soup in the frying pan filled with steak juice.
Continuously stir, bringing to a rolling boil.
Pour over steaks.

buttered spaghetti goes great with this dish.

Venison steak 3

3 pound slab boneless sirloin
1 teaspoon salt
1 teaspoon black peppercorn
English mustard

Cut sirloin into 2 inch thick pieces.
Rinse off and rub meat with a damp cloth. Rub meat with salt, pepper, and a smidgen of English mustard. Preheat boiler for 10 minutes at a high temperature.

Place steak 5 inches below the heat on a oiled grill (prevents sticking). Cook both sides approximately 7 min. each side. Place big slabs of butter on top of steaks. Serve on preheated plates.

Mandarin Venison

2 lb. venison steak, thinly sliced
1 tbsp. oil
1 small onion, finely chopped
¼ tbsp. garlic powder
1 tbsp. chili powder
1 tbsp. salt
1 tbsp. plum jelly or jam
1 tbsp. vinegar
2 bouillon cubes
1 tbsp. cornstarch
1 cup rice

Brown Venison in oil. Add onion, garlic, and chili powder. Add salt, jelly, vinegar, bouillon cubes and 2 cups water. Cover with tight lid. Simmer until meat is tender, about 1 hour. Thicken with cornstarch.

Cook rice. Serve rice topped with meat.

Venison Scalloppini

2 ½ lb. venison steak
½ cup vinegar
½ Seasoned flour
2 medium onions, peeled and sliced
1 tsp. sugar
1 4-0z. can mushrooms
1 ¼ cup tomato puree

Cover venison with water and vinegar. Soak overnight. Drain 'n' roll in seasoned flour. Fry until brown, turn, and add onions. Brown other side. Add remaining ingredients with 1 ¼ cups water.

Place in casserole dish and bake at 3500 for 2 hours.

Venison Steak Piquant

2 to 3 large 1" thick venison steaks
Dash, (meat tenderizer)
Flour
Salt & pepper
¾ tsp. garlic salt
1 medium large onion, diced
2 bay leaves
1 tbsp. Worcestershire sauce
2 4-oz. cans mushrooms

Add tenderizer and pierce with fork.
Pound flour into steaks. Brown in frying pan.
Add salt & pepper to taste; add garlic salt,
onion, bay leaves, Worcestershire sauce.
mushrooms and 1 ½ cups water. Cover and
simmer 2 ½ to 3 hours until tender. Remove
steak when done. Make gravy with remaining
liquid. Add more water during cooking if
needed.

Venison Chow Mein

3 tbsp. bacon fat
1 cup venison, cut into ½ inch cubes
½ onion, finely chopped
1 ½ cup celery, cut into small pieces
½ cup water
½ tsp. salt
3 tbsp. cornstarch
1/8 tsp. pepper
1 tbsp. brown sugar
1 tbsp. soy sauce
½ can bean sprouts
9 8-oz. cans bamboo sprouts
1 8-oz. can water chestnuts

Heat fat in skillet. Add meat and onion. Fry quickly until meat is well seared. Add celery, water and salt, then cover and boil for 4 minutes. Combine cornstarch, pepper, brown sugar and soy sauce, then add 2 tbsp. water, Mix until smooth. Add meat mixture and vegetables. Bring to slow boil, stirring occasionally. Serve over noodles.

Venison Ragout

2 tbsp. butter or margarine
2 tbsp. all-purpose flour
1 cup chicken bouillon
1 tbsp. Worcestershire
1 tbsp. currant jelly
2 cups 1 inch cubes of cooked venison
Salt & pepper to taste

Brown butter in skillet. Add flour and continue to cook until flour browns. Add bouillon, stir constantly until thickened. Add Worcestershire and jelly, then cook over low heat, stirring constantly, until jelly is melted. Add meat and seasonings. Cook on low heat until meat is heated through

4
SWISS STEAK

Venison Swiss Steak 1

4 ½ pound steaks
1/3 cup all-purpose flour
1 teaspoon garlic salt
1/8 tablespoon paprika
1/8 teaspoon freshly ground black
pepper
3 tablespoons cooking oil
¼ cup chopped parsley
¼ cup minced onion
1 can mushroom soup
1 can water
½ pound well sized egg noodles
2 tablespoon butter
½ pound fresh mushrooms
1 cup sour cream

Continued on next pg.

Add garlic salt, paprika, and black pepper together. Press into both sides of the meat. Heat oil in skillet over medium heat. Brown steaks and minced onion. Add mushroom soup and bring up to a light boil. Cover and simmer approximately one hour, or until your fork easily pierces the meat. Cook noodles according to directions on package and then dry. Add melted butter to noodles. Place steaks over top and keep warm. With a straining spoon or slotted spatula, scoop out mushrooms and pour over top of steak and noodles. Sprinkle each serving with chopped parsley.

Remaining liquid from skillet can be used as a creamy topping for additional servings, or for another dish.

Venison Swiss Steak 2

2 venison steaks
1 can cream mushroom soup
2 large sliced onions
Salt
Pepper
Worcestershire sauce
½ cup water

Cut prepared steaks into serving portions. Place steaks in large skillet and add ½ cup water

Simmer meat approximately 10 minutes on each side. Add in remaining ingredients and, if need be, a little more water. Simmer on low heat for 1 hr. or until tender, occasionally turning over to prevent sticking.

Venison Swiss Steak 3

6 tablespoons flour
½ teaspoons salt
¼ teaspoon pepper
2 pounds round venison steak
2 cups cooked tomatoes
1 large onion, sliced
1 bay leaf, crushed
1 small can mushrooms
¼ cup fat

Combined salt, pepper, and flour. Cover both sides of steak. Melt fat in skillet. Brown both sides of steaks. Remove steaks from skillet. Set oven temperature at 300°. Place steaks in a deep bake pan. Add tomatoes, onion and bay leaf, then cover. Bake in oven for 1 hr 30 min or until tender. Uncover and add mushrooms. Bake an additional 30 minutes. Cook leftover sauce to a rich thickness, then pour over steaks.

Venison Swiss Steak 4

> 1 teaspoon salt
> 1 teaspoon pepper
> 2 pounds round venison
> 1 15 ounce can of tomato sauce
> 2 4 ounce cans of mushroom pieces and
>   stems

Salt and pepper each side of steaks. Fry in oil until done. Cover with tomato sauce and ½ can water. Simmer an additional 20 minutes. Add mushrooms and simmer an additional 15 minutes.

If desired, add 1 diced onion at the same time of adding mushrooms.

6 venison steaks, tenderized (about 1/2
  pound each)
½ cup flour
½ tsp. salt and pepper
3 tbsp cooking oil
2 large onions, cut into ¼ inch thick
  slices
4 cups of stewed tomatoes
1 tsp paprika

Preheat the oven to 325 ° F. Combine the
flour, salt, pepper, and paprika. Cover venison
steaks in the seasoned flour mixture, coating
both sides. In a frying pan, add oil over
medium heat.   Brown both sides of the steaks.
Place the browned venison steaks in a
dutch oven. Add the remaining ingredients.
Cover the dish and place in the oven, baking 2
to 3 hrs, or until the meat is tender.
Serve over garlic mashed potatoes.

Stuffed Slices of Venison

    2 lbs. venison, sliced thin
    2 tbsp. boiled ham, chopped
    2 tbsp. Parmesan cheese, grated
    6 tbsp. butter
    1 onion, minced
    2 tbsp. parsley, minced
    1 pinch thyme
    2 cups bread crumbs
    Salt & pepper

Make stuffing: In one pan, brown the bread crumbs in butter. In another pan saute' onions, parsley and ham. Combine these ingredients and add egg yolks, cheese, thyme, salt and pepper. Mix well. Place 1 tablespoon of stuffing on each slice. Roll or turn in edges, skewer, dip each slice in melted butter and bake at 350°F. until done.

5
CHOPS

Barbecued Venison Chops with Savory Butter

4 venison chops
½ cup soft butter
1 tbsp. onion, minced
½ cup chili sauce
½ cup lemon juice
1 tbsp. parsley, minced
2 tsp. dry mustard
1 tsp. salt

Blend mustard, onion, parsley and butter, and shape into roll. Then chill until hard. Combine chili sauce, lemon juice and salt, and dip chops in mixture. Broil chops for 45 minutes 12 to 14 inches above flame-less coals. Turn chops once, about 20 minutes before they are done.

If desired, place in a sliced butter roll.

Venison Chops Parmesan

8 venison chops
1 tbsp. butter
2 medium onions, peeled,
quartered, & sliced
1 tbsp. shortening
Salt & pepper
1 tbsp. Worcestershire
1 cup beef bouillon
8 slices French bread, toasted
1 cup sour cream
3 tbsp. grated Parmesan cheese

Trim fat from chops. Melt butter and saute onions until they are limp. Remove onions and add shortening. Brown chops on both sides and sprinkle with salt and pepper to taste. Top with onions and bouillon. Simmer covered, 15 to 30 minutes (until tender).

Arrange toast on individual plates, top each slice with a chop and keep warm. Add sour cream and Worcestershire to pan drippings. Stir until mixed while heating. Pour over chops and sprinkle with Parmesan cheese.

Venison Chops

Heat ¼ cup oil in skillet and 1 clove garlic sliced. Lightly brown clove, then add chops and brown.

Add:
1 can stewed tomatoes
½ tsp. salt
¼ tsp. chopped parsley
¼ tsp. oregano
3 medium carrots, cut in pieces
1 green pepper, diced
1 can mushrooms

Cover skillet and simmer ½ hour or until the chops are tender. If mixture over-thickens, add more water. The chops become very tender.

Broiled Venison Chops

6 venison chops
½ cup oil
¼ cup vinegar
1 tsp. salt
1 tsp. sugar
Pepper

Mix oil with vinegar, salt, and pepper. Marinate chops in this mixture for 2 to 3 hours. Place under broiler and broil steaks to desired done-ness.

6
CUTLETS

Venison Cutlets

      4 ½ lb. venison cutlets
      2 large eggs
      5 tbsp. water
      3 cups fine bread crumbs
      1 cup sifted flour
      ½ stick butter or margarine
      Fresh lemon juice

Cut cutlets ½ inch thick and hammer with cleaver, until very thin. Beat eggs and water. Dip cutlets in this. Then mix bread crumbs and flour. Roll venison in this mixture. Let dry ¾ hour. Saute cutlets in butter or margarine on low heat, until they are golden. Sprinkle lightly with lemon juice and serve.

Venison Cutlets 1

2 lbs. venison
½ cup sour cream
1 cup flour
2 tbsp. butter
1 palm of celery
Pinch salt
Worcestershire sauce
Salt & pepper
Bay leaf

Roll cutlets in flour seasoned with salt and pepper. In frying pan, melt butter over medium heat. Brown meat on both sides. When venison is well browned, pour sour cream over cutlets and season with remaining ingredients. Cover and cook over low flame until tender. (about 1 hour).

Venison Cutlets 2

2 lb Venison roast or loin (sliced thin)
2 eggs
½ milk
1 cup flour
Salt & pepper
¼ cup vegetable oil

Slice Venison thinly. Pound both sides of thinly sliced venison with meat mallet. Place on plate.

1st dish mix:
2 eggs
½ cup milk
2nd dish mix:
Flour
Salt & Pepper mixed

Dip venison into egg & milk mix, then dip into bowl of mixed flour until completely covered. In deep frying pan add ¼ cup vegetable oil. Heat oil until hot. Slowly drop seasoned venison into hot oil (approx. 2 to 5 min. each piece).

Eat cold or hot.

Texas Fried Venison

2 lbs. venison, cut into pieces
¼ cup flour
1 tsp. salt
Fresh ground pepper
3 tbsp. bacon fat
1 piece celery, cut up
3 medium onions, sliced
1 tbsp. Worcestershire sauce
2 cups tomatoes
Noodles

Cut venison into serving size pieces. Mix flour with salt and pepper to taste. Coat venison with flour mixture. Heat bacon fat in skillet, then brown venison on both sides. Add celery and onions. Saute till brown. Add Worcestershire sauce and tomatoes. Cover and cook for 1 to 2 hours or until tender. Cook noodles, drain, and serve with venison.

French-Fried Venison

2" to 4" strips of Venison
2 eggs (beaten)
1 cup cracked bread crumbs

Cut venison into strips of 4" x 2" Dip in beaten egg and then roll in fine cracker crumbs. Chill ½ hr.

Preheat deep frier to 370°. Put in the strips of meat. Fry until golden brown, then spread on crumpled paper toweling to drain. Salt strips and serve hot.

Or if you'd prefer baking:

Cut strips the same as before. Dip in melted butter or margarine. Spread in a shallow pan and bake at 400°, turning occasionally until golden brown. Sprinkle with salt and serve.

Venison Sticks

1 lb Venison cut into 4" x 2" strips
1 cup Butter or Margarine
dash of Garlic salt
dash of Paprika
dash of MSG
dash of Parsley flakes
dash of Parmesan cheese

Cut venison steak into 4" x 2" strips. Dip in melted butter or margarine. Lay in a single layer in a shallow greased pan. Dust with garlic salt, paprika, mono-sodium glutamate, and parsley flakes.

Turning occasionally, bake at 400° for 15 min. or until the sticks are golden brown. Sprinkle with Parmesan cheese and serve hot.

7
ROAST

Venison Pot Roast

1 cup dry red wine
1 cup water
1 ½ tsp. salt
2 bay leaves
10 whole cloves
5 whole allspice
2 chili peppers
1 large onion, sliced
1 5-6 lb. venison roast (any cut)
2 tbsp. bacon fat

Marinade:

Combine all ingredients except meat and bacon fat. Put meat in deep plastic container. Pour marinade over meat. Cover and marinate in refrigerator for 2 days. Drain and reserve marinade. Dry meat. Strain marinade. In Dutch oven, brown meat on all sides in the bacon fat. Add ½ cup reserved marinade. Cover and simmer over low heat for 2 to 3 hours or until tender. Add more marinade to prevent sticking. Remove pot roast to hot serving dish and slice thickly. Keep hot. Make gravy in the usual manner. Pour gravy over meat. Serve over wild rice or buttered noodles.

Venison Pot Roast With Vegetables

Flour
1/8 tsp. pepper
½ tsp. salt
3 to 4 lbs. venison, wiped dry
5 carrots, quartered
5 potatoes, quartered
1 turnip, quartered and sliced
5 onions, peeled and quartered
1 small cabbage, cut in wedges

Combine flour, pepper, and salt. Coat meat in mixture. Saute the meat and keep warm on the side. In a heavy pan or Dutch oven, add I cup water to cover. Cook very slowly until tender. Add vegetables, placing wedges of cabbage around. Another cup of water may need to be added. Make gravy of pan juices. Serve with meat.

Venison Roast

¼ lb. butter
Juice of ½ lemon
1 ½ tsp. salt
¼ tsp. pepper
1 tsp. Worcestershire sauce
1 clove of garlic, sliced
1 cup red wine
1 6 to 8 lb. roast

Combine first 7 ingredients. Brush venison thoroughly with sauce. Let stand for 2 to 3 hours at room temperature. Brown at 475° in oven. Then cover and reduce heat to 300°. Roast for about 6 hours. Baste occasionally with sauce during cooking time.

Venison Shanks With Rosemary

> 6 slices venison from upper shank, cut
>   1" thick
> Olive oil
> 6 medium potatoes, peeled & halved
> Salt & pepper
> Basting sauce recipe (below)

Rub meat with olive oil and place in a large flat roasting pan. Brown in preheated oven at 500°F, turning once to brown both sides. Place potatoes around meat and sprinkle both with salt and pepper. Reduce heat to low at 325°F and roast for 1 hour, basting frequently with basting sauce.

8
STEW

Venison Stew with Wine

    4 1bs. venison
    4 tbsp. flour
    2 tsp. seasoned salt
    6-8 tbsp. butter
    2 cups burgundy
    2 cups beef bouillon fr.
    ½ cup dry white wine
    6 carrots
    6 stalks celery with leaves
    2 medium onions
    2 cloves garlic
    3-4 bay leaves
    2 tbsp. parsley
    ½ tsp. chives

Chervil and thyme (mixture)
    Salt and Pepper to taste
    1 lb. sliced mushrooms
    1 cup sour cream
    2 tsp. paprika
    Small potatoes Pre-cooked to your
      liking

Continued on next pg.

Cut venison into bite-size cubes. Put flour and seasoned salt in a plastic bag, shaking to coat the pieces of meat. Melt butter (add more as needed) in a stew pot over medium heat. Brown the floured venison chunks in batches of 12 or 15 pieces at a time, then put them aside as they become done. Don't overcook. Just brown the pieces.

When all the pieces are done, put them in the pot. Add burgundy, beef bouillon, white wine and bring to a low boil. Add sliced carrots, diced celery with leaves, sliced onions, pressed garlic, bay leaves, chopped fresh parsley, mixture of chives, chervil and thyme into pot. Add salt and fresh-ground pepper. Cover and simmer for an hour.

Add mushrooms and some pre-cooked potato balls and simmer for 20 minutes more. Stir in sour cream and paprika, then simmer for another 10 minutes. Add the small potatoes and wine to your liking.

Venison Stew #1

2 lb. Venison cut into 1inch cubes
4 tbsp. bacon drippings
1 tsp. garlic salt
1 tsp. Worcestershire sauce
1 ½ tsp. salt
½ tsp. black pepper
1 cup chopped onions
4 medium potatoes, cubed
6 medium size carrots, sliced
1 green pepper, chopped
2 cups sliced celery
3 tbsp. all-purpose flour
¼ cup cold water

Brown venison cubes in hot bacon drippings in heavy Dutch oven. Add water to cover, seasonings and onion. Cover and simmer about 2 hours. Add potatoes, carrots, pepper, and celery. Cook about 20 minutes or until tender. Then dissolve flour in ¼ cup cold water and stir into stew. Cook about 5 minutes longer and serve hot.

Venison Stew #2

1 ½ lbs. venison cubes
½ cup sifted flour
1 ½ cups red table wine
1 (8 oz.) can whole onions
1 cup frozen peas
½ cup sour cream
½ pkg. pastry mix
1 tsp. cornstarch
2 tbsp. shortening
¼ tsp. pepper
1 tsp. dry mustard
½ tsp. paprika
1 ½ tsp. salt

Blend flour, salt, pepper, mustard, and paprika, then use mix to coat meat. Brown slowly in hot shortening. Add wine, re-heat to a boil, and pour contents into baking dish. Cover tightly and bake at 300DF for 1 ½ to 2 hours, until venison is very tender. Drain onions and separate peas (they don't need to be completely thawed). Stir cornstarch into sour cream. Combine onions, peas, and sour cream with meat and mix. Prepare pastry mix and roll to fit top of dish, fluting edges and slashing to allow steam to escape. Brown in 400°F oven 20 minutes.

Venison Stew #3

3 lbs. venison cut into 1"x1" cubes
Salt
1 clove garlic, minced
5 quartered potatoes
½ cup diced celery
1 cup diced carrots
1 tbsp. flour & butter per cup of stock
12 oz. pack frozen peas
3 tbsp. lemon juice or wine vinegar
1 tbsp. chopped parsley
1 cup diced onions
Boiling water to cover.

Seasonings tied into cloth for bouquet:
Several cloves
6 crushed peppercorns
Bit of ginger root
Small piece stick cinnamon
Few sprigs parsley
Few branches celery leaves

Put venison in pot, add salt, cover with boiling water, and simmer. Add seasonings bouquet. Simmer gently for 25 minutes. Remove seasonings. Add minced garlic, potatoes, celery, onions, and carrots. Cover and cook over low flame 40 minutes.

Continued on next pg.

Pour off stock. Add 1 tbsp. flour and butter for each cup of stock. Cook until thickened. Add peas. Cook 5 minutes. Add lemon juice and parsley. Pour gravy over meat and vegetables and serve.

Venison Stew #4

2 lbs. venison
Bacon fat
Salt & pepper
½ tsp. ground cloves
1 onion, cut fine
½ cup ketchup
1 tsp. vinegar
I cup red wine

Brown carefully trimmed, small pieces
of venison in fry pan with hot bacon. Salt and
pepper. Then add ground cloves, onion,
ketchup, vinegar, and red wine. Cook until
meat is tender.

NOTE: you can mix venison with beef or pork.

Hunters' Stew

1 ½ lbs. venison stew meat, cubed
Flour
2 tbsp. cooking oil
1 onion, coarsely chopped
1 clove garlic, minced
1 tsp. salt
1/8 tsp. pepper
2 cups water
¾ cup dry red wine
1 beef bouillon cube
6 carrots, cut in to 2 inch strips
2 stalks celery, cut into 2 inch strips
1 cup fresh or frozen cranberries
1 tsp. sugar
1 tbsp. steak sauce
2 tsp. Hungarian paprika
4 juniper berries (optional)
2 whole cloves
1 bay leaf
Cornstarch

Continued on next pg.

In a Dutch oven, brown onion and garlic. Coat stew meat in seasoned flour and brown in the hot oil. Add wine, water, and bouillon, then bring to a boil. Cover and simmer for 1 ¼ hours. Add carrots, celery, cranberries, sugar, steak sauce, paprika, juniper berries, cloves, and bay leaf. Cover and simmer another 45 minutes until vegetables are tender. Thicken broth to taste by mixing cornstarch with a little cold water.

Fancy Venison Stew

3 or 4 lbs. venison
1 cup flour
Salt & pepper
1 lb. fresh sliced mushrooms
1 cup chopped onions
1 green pepper, chopped fine
¼ lb. butter
1 can tomatoes
½ bottle red wine
Canned beef bouillon

Cut venison into 1" cubes. Coat with flour, salt, and pepper. In heavy iron pot, saute mushrooms, green pepper, and onion. When lightly golden brown, remove from pot, turn up heat, and sear meat in butter and juices until meat cubes are browned on all sides.

More butter may be required. Return sauteed vegetables to pot with meat. Add tomatoes, and enough beef bouillon to cover. Simmer for 2 hours. Add wine, and bring to boil. Lower heat and simmer for ½ hour longer.

Venison Crock-pot Stew

1 lb Venison, cubed
3 or 4 medium potatoes
½ lb carrots
1 medium onion diced
1 can green beans
1 small can mushrooms
Salt & pepper to taste
1 can brown gravy
1 small can water
¼ cup vegetable oil

Pour ¼ cup vegetable oil in frying pan, brown cubed venison. Cut potatoes & carrots to bite size. Dice medium onion. Add everything to crock-pot. Cover & cook 4 hrs at low temp.

If you like tomatoes, add ½ can stewed tomatoes.

9
CHOPMEAT

Ground Venison

      Venison amount (lbs) to desire
      Beef fat (No more than 25% of total
            weight of Venison)
      Seasonings blend: (For each pound of -
            - ground Venison and Beef Fat)
      ½ teaspoon of salt
      1/8 teaspoon of ground black pepper
      ¼ teaspoon of mustard
      Shredded cheddar cheese, ½ cup to
      each pound of burger
      Lemon juice (if desired)

      Remove any wild fat. Add 25% Beef Fat. Grind Venison with Beef Fat. Mix measured seasonings with ground Venison, then form in to patties and/or meat loaf.

Best pan broiled without the addition of any butter or margarine.

Deer Burgers

2 lbs. ground venison
¼ lb. ground beef fat
1 chopped onion
4 slices fresh bread broken into small
   pieces or bread crumbs
Seasoning (to taste)

Mix the venison, fat, onion, and bread. Add seasoning. Make into patties and fry or broil.

Venison Burgers

    salt & pepper
    1 egg
    1 medium onion
    ¼ cup bread crumbs
    ¼ cup ketchup

    Form into ¼ lb. burgers. Fry over
medium heat to liking.

Venison Meatballs

2 lbs. venison, ground
1 medium onion, chopped
1 garlic clove, peeled & minced
1 cup tomato juice
I cup dry bread crumbs
1 tsp. Worcestershire
1 ½ tsp. salt
½ tsp. pepper
Water
All-purpose flour
Herbed Wild Rice

Mix together all ingredients thoroughly, except water and flour. Form into balls the size of a golf ball. Brown them in shortening and transfer to a 2 quart kettle. Pour a small amount of water into the skillet and heat, scraping the bottom to remove all particles. Pour over meatballs and add enough water to cover, then cover 'n' simmer for about 45 min.

Pour off the liquid and measure. Mix a smooth paste of flour 1 ½ tbsp. flour for each cup of liquid and water; measuring 2 tbsp. Water. Gradually add the hot liquid, stirring constantly, and cook until thickened.
Serve over Herbed Wild Rice.

Venison Meatballs 2

        1 lbs venison
        2 eggs
        bread crumbs
        ketchup
        spaghetti sauce (your choice)
        salt & pepper
        spice to desire

    Mix above ingredient together. Roll into
meat balls. Place in pan with spaghetti sauce.
Simmer in deep frying pan about ½ hr till
done.

Hunter's Chili

1 lb. of venison
1 lb. moose scraps
1 lb. sm. red chili beans or kidney beans
½ tsp. baking soda
1 tbsp. salt
¼ cup shortening
1 large onion, chopped
4-6 tbsp. chili powder
2 tbsp. all-purpose flour
3 garlic cloves, peeled & minced
4 tsp. crumbled dried oregano
2 tsp. ground cumin seed
1 ½ tsp. crumbled dried sage or
    ¾ tsp. ground sage

Soak beans overnight in water. In the morning, add baking soda and bring to a boil. Boil for 10 min. Drain and rinse. Cover beans with water, add salt, and bring to a boil. Trim fat & tendons from meat and cut into small cubes. Brown in shortening, then add to the beans. Cook onion in remaining shortening until golden brown, stirring occasionally. Add chili powder and flour, then mix. Add to beans and meat. Add remaining ingredients, then cover and simmer for 4 hrs, stirring occasionally, adding more water if necessary.

Texas Venison Chili

2 lbs. coarsely ground venison
¼ cup vegetable oil
1 cup chopped onions
2 cloves minced garlic
1 large green pepper, cut into strips
3 tbsp. chili powder
2 tsp. sugar
3 ½ cups whole tomatoes
1 cup tomato sauce
1 cup water
½ tsp. salt
2 cups cooked kidney beans

Brown venison in oil. Add onions, garlic, and green pepper. Cook 5 minutes, stirring constantly. Add next 6 ingredients and simmer 1 ½ hours. If thicker chili is desired, stir in 1 tbsp. flour mixed with 2 tbsp. water. Just before serving, add 2 cups cooked kidney beans.

Grandma's Venison Chilli

2 lbs ground venison
2 medium onions
2 can red beans
1 46 oz. can tomato juice
½ can chili powder
¼ cup diced red or green peppers

Brown ground venison meat with onions. In a deep pot, add 3 cans red beans & the tomato juice. Add browned ground meat with onions, then salt to taste. Add ¼ cup diced red &/or green peppers. Set flame to simmer. Cook till done (about 45 min).

Venison Meatloaf

    2 lbs ground Venison
    2 eggs
    ½ cup bread crumbs
    ½ cup ketchup
    salt & pepper to taste
    1 medium onion
    ¼ cup green or red peppers

    Mix above contents together. Form a loaf in a loaf pan. Pour ketchup over top for design. Place in oven, and bake at 350°F for 45 min. or till done.

10
OVEN

Dutch Oven Venison

4 lb. venison round steak
1 cup seasoned flour
3 tbsp. shortening
4 large onions, sliced

Slice steaks thinly, then pound with meat hammer. Smother in seasoned flour. Fry in hot skillet with shortening. Fry a few pieces at a time until brown. Lay steaks in alternate pattern with onion slices in Dutch oven, then cover. Bake at 3500 in oven for 1 hour. Add a small amount of water from time to time to keep from sticking.

Venison With Sour Cream

¼ cup fat
2 lb. venison, cut into pieces
1 clove of garlic
1 cup diced celery
½ cup minced onion
1 cup diced carrots
1 tsp. salt
Pepper to taste
2 cup water
4 tbsp. butter
4 tbsp. flour
1 cup sour cream

Melt fat in heavy frying pan. Add meat and garlic. Brown on all sides and arrange in dish. Put vegetables in remaining fat. Cook for 2 minutes. Add salt, pepper, and water filled to cover meat.

Bake in slow oven until meat is tender. Melt butter in frying pan; stir in flour. Add the water that meat was cooked in. Boil until thick. Add sour cream and more salt, Pour over meat and vegetables. May be served with buttered noodles and currant jelly.

Oven Venison

    2 lbs. venison, cubed
    1 can cream mushroom soup
    1 envelope onion soup mix
    1 ½ can of water
    8 oz. canned, sliced mushrooms
    3 tbsp. margarine

Place venison in a 9"x13"x2" pan. In a 1 quart bowl, mix the canned mushroom soup, onion soup mix, and water. Pour mixture over venison and place pieces of margarine on top. Cover pan with aluminum foil. Set pan on middle rack of oven and bake at 350°F for 1 hour 15 minutes. When meat is done, uncover pan and add sliced mushrooms. Return pan to oven for 5 minutes to heat mushrooms. Serve over rice.

Rice for Above Dish:

1 ½ cups raw, fine egg noodles, crushed
4 tbsp. cooking oil
1 ½ cups raw rice (washed not
precooked)
3 cups water
½ tsp. salt

Pour oil into a 4 quart pot and heat on
low flame. Add crushed noodles to oil just
until they turn light brown. Immediately add
washed rice, water, salt, and stir. Cover and
cook for 12 to 14 minutes or until rice is soft.

Venison Loaf

1 ½ lbs. ground venison
2 eggs
½ cup oatmeal
1 tsp. poultry seasoning
1 tbsp. chopped onion
½ cup canned milk
1 tsp. salt
¼ tsp. pepper
½ cup ketchup

Combine all ingredients except ketchup. Pack loosely in 9"x5"x3" bake pan. Spread over with ketchup. Bake for 1 hour at 3500.

Venison Meat Loaf

1 lb. ground venison
½ tbsp. minced onion
1/3 lb. ground pork
1 egg
1 cup milk
½ cup dried bread crumbs
1 ½ tsp. salt

Mix onion and pork thoroughly. Add egg, milk, bread crumbs, salt, and onion. Place in a greased deep pan. Bake for 1 hour at 3500

Smothered Venison # 1

3 lbs. venison, round or rump
salt & pepper
flour
1 tsp. celery seed
2 tbsp. prepared mustard or horseradish
1 cup strained tomatoes
¼ cup fat

Season the venison with salt and pepper and roll in flour. Place in melted fat in a Dutch oven and brown on all sides. Add the celery seed, prepared mustard or horseradish, and strained tomatoes.

Cover and simmer 3 hours or until tender.

Smothered Venison # 2

2 lbs. venison, round
1 cup strained tomatoes
flour
melted fat
2 tbsp. prepared mustard or horseradish
1 tsp. celery seed
Salt & pepper

Season the venison with salt and pepper. Roll in flour. Place in Dutch oven and brown on all sides in melted fat. Add the celery seeds, mustard or horseradish and strained tomatoes. Cover and simmer about 3 hours.

Venison Ragout

3 lbs. venison sirloin, cut in ½" cubes
1 tsp. salt
¼ tsp. pepper
3 tbsp. flour
¼ cup olive oil
3 onions, quartered
2 cups red wine
1 to 2 cans of tomatoes
2 cloves of garlic, crushed
1 tsp. powdered ginger

Coat venison with salt, pepper, and flour; brown slowly in olive oil, and place in large Dutch oven. Saute onions until transparent. Add wine, tomatoes, garlic, and ginger. Cover. Simmer for 4 hrs or until meat is tender.

Venison Ragout with Onions

3 lbs. top round of venison, cut into
   medium-sized cubes
2 ½ tbsp. butter
3 tbsp. dry sherry (warmed)
36 small white onions
1 tbsp. tomato paste
2 tbsp. meat glaze
3 ½ tbsp. flour
1 ½ cups beef stock
2 cups dry red wine
2 small bay leaves
14 small white mushrooms
Salt & pepper
2 tbsp. finely chopped fresh parsley

Continued on next pg.

Saute the venison in hot melted butter, turning often until brown. Pour the warm sherry over it and stir well. Then take the meat from the frying pan. Add the onions to the butter and sherry. Brown, stirring often so that the onions do not burn. Stir in the tomato paste, meat glaze, and flour. Blending until smooth. Then add the beef stock and stir until the mixture begins to simmer. Add ½ cup of red wine, venison pieces, bay leaves, and mushrooms, season with salt & pepper. Stir well while simmering slowly for 1 ½ hrs. or until venison is tender. Add the rest of the red wine during the cooking. Sprinkle parsley over top. Serve with hot buttered noodles and endive salad. Topped with a good Burgundy wine.

North Wood's Venison Casserole

2 lbs. venison or moose meat, cubed
1 pkg. dry onion soup mix
1 can mushroom soup
2 fresh tomatoes

Place meat in casserole. Add onion soup mix, mushroom soup mix, and tomato. Cover and Bake for 2 hrs at 325°.

Barbecued Venison Ribs

  3 to 4 1bs. venison ribs
  1 lemon, sliced
  1 large onion, sliced
  1 cup ketchup
  1/3 cup Worcestershire sauce
  1 tsp. chili powder
  1 tsp. salt
  4 or 5 dashes Tabasco sauce
  2 cups water

  Place ribs in shallow pan. Place a slice of unpeeled lemon and a thin slice of onion on each piece. Roast at 4000 for 30 min. Combine remaining ingredients, and bring to boil. Pour over ribs. Continue baking at 3500 until tender. Baste ribs every 20 minutes.

Luau Venison

5 lb. deer meat, cubed
¾ cup flour
¾ cup cooking oil
1 cup water
2 ½ cans pineapple chunks, drained
3 large white onions, cut in thick slices
1 cup celery, cut into medium chunks
3 green peppers, cubed
¼ cup dark brown sugar
¼ cup soy sauce
2 tbsp. sliced fresh ginger

Cover meat in flour. Fry in oil until brown. Add water and cover. Cook until tender. Remove meat 'n' thicken gravy with a dash of cornstarch. Put pineapple, onions, celery, and peppers in roaster.
Mix sugar, soy sauce, and ginger into gravy, then pour over vegetables. Add meat. Cover. Bake at 350 for 30 min or until vegetables are tender but not soft. Lightly mix ingredients; serve over steamed rice.

Venison Stroganoff

2 lbs. venison round steak, cut ¾" thick
2 tbsp. shortening
1 large onion, peeled and chopped
½ tsp. salt
1/8 tsp. pepper
1 can (10-1/2 oz.) beef bouillon
¼ lb. fresh mushrooms
2 tbsp. butter or margarine
2 tbsp. all-purpose flour
1 tsp. prepared mustard
1 cup sour cream

Remove bone and fat from meat. Cut into strips about ¼" wide and 1 ½" long. Brown meat in shortening in a skillet. Transfer meat to a 2-quart casserole dish. Add onion, salt, and pepper. Heat bouillon in skillet. Pour over meat and bake, covered, at 350° for 1 ½ hrs, stirring occasionally.

Wash and slice mushrooms and saute in butter until golden. Stir in flour. Drain the liquid from the meat and add gradually while stirring. Cook over low heat, stirring constantly, until smooth and thickened. Add mustard and sour cream. Blend well. Pour over meat. Serve over cooked rice.

Venison Roast

1 Venison Roast
½ lb beef fat
2 cups red wine
1 cup garlic oil

Soak strips of beef fat overnight in a red wine & garlic oil blend. Preheat oven at 300°. Bake 12 min. per pound (don't cover). If you are using a meat thermometer, insert it in the thickest part, not touching any bone. A temperature of 130° meat is now rare, 140° medium, and 150° well done.

Setting the fatter side of the meat, (if any), up and the bony side down (if possible), baste with melted butter or margarine every 15 min. laying strips of beef fat over the roast. When done cooking, sprinkle salt to flavor.

Sweet 'n' Sour Venison Tenderloin

4 lbs. venison tenderloin
1 medium-sized onion, thinly sliced
1 clove of garlic, minced
½ stick butter or margarine
3 tbsp. lemon juice
1 tbsp. brown sugar
1 tbsp. Worcestershire sauce
2 tsp. salt
8 sliced medium sized mushrooms

Prepare sauce by slowly sauteing the onion and garlic in the butter, until the onion is translucent only and the grease un-browned. Then mix in lemon juice, brown sugar, Worcestershire sauce, salt, and mushrooms. Set the tenderloin in a greased pan and spoon the sauce over it. Cook uncovered at 400 for about 45 minutes or until done to your own personal satisfaction, basting occasionally and testing for done-ness. Slice the meat and serve hot with the sauce.

Split Stuffed Pepper

1 lb venison, ground
6 Italian light green peppers
2 eggs
½ cup instant rice (add more in need)
1 medium onion, chopped fine
½ cup red peppers
salt & pepper to taste
Spaghetti sauce with mushrooms or
   without

Mix above ingredients except spaghetti sauce. Slice Italian light green pepper in half, length-wise and remove seeds. Fill each half with venison mix. Lay meat-side up in a baking pan. Pour spaghetti sauce over to desired amount. Cook in oven 35min to 45 min. at 350°F.

11
GRILLED

Grilled Loin

6 venison loin chops
2 tbsp. melted butter
6 slices bacon
Salt, pepper

Baste loin strips with butter. Wrap each strip with one slice bacon. Place meat on grill over medium hot coals. Grill, turning frequently. Cook 4 to 5 minutes on each side for medium done-ness. Add salt and pepper to taste.

Spicy Barbecued Roast Venison

    4 lb. venison roast of leg, rump or
      shoulder
    2 tbsp. olive oil
    1 cup chili sauce
    1 cup water
    2 tbsp. vinegar
    1 tbsp. Worcestershire
    1 tsp. salt
    ¼ tsp. pepper
    1/8 tsp. each of celery, salt, ground
      cinnamon & ground cloves
    1 small onion, finely chopped
    ½ lemon, thinly sliced
    ½ cup currant jelly

Brown roast on all sides in olive oil, then place in a roasting pan. Add all the remaining ingredients, except jelly, into the pan of juices and re-heat until boiling. Scrape the bottom of pan to loosen all particles. Pour sauce over meat and roast in preheated oven at 350°F, until meat reaches the desired degree of tenderness (about 1 ½ hours for rare, 2 to 2 ½ hours for medium or well done). Baste occasionally with sauce and add more water if necessary. Remove meat to serving platter.

Continued on next pg.

Strain basting sauce, add jelly, and cook over moderate heat, (stirring constantly) until jelly is melted and sauce becomes smooth. Serve hot and spoon over sliced meat.

12
INNARDS & SPECIALS

Pickled Venison Heart

    1 venison heart
    2 bay leaves
    Salt & pepper
    3 parts water to 1 part vinegar
    1 small onion, sliced

    Place heart in a large saucepan. Add
enough water to cover the heart. Add a little
salt and bay leaves, then bring to a boil. Lower
heat, cover and simmer until tender. When
heart is tender, drain, cool, and then slice
thinly. Place the slices in a bowl with the onion
and water / vinegar mixture (enough to cover
the meat). Add salt and pepper to taste. Store
in refrigerator for 3 to 4 hrs. Dry meat with
paper toweling before eating.

Venison Heart

1 heart of Venison
1 to 2 onions, chopped
Olive oil
½ cup chopped celery
1 tsp. salt
¼ tsp. pepper
1 to 2 cloves of garlic
1 tsp. Butter
2 small cans tomato sauce
½ cup rice

Brown onion in oil. Remove membrane from heart and cut into cubes. Add celery, chopped heart, salt, pepper, garlic, and butter to browned onion. Add tomato sauce. Simmer until tender, adding more liquid if needed. Serve over rice.

Heart of Venison 2

1 Venison Heart

Cook heart in boiling water, adding a little salt. Allow to cool, and cut as desired.

Fried Liver

> 1 Venison liver
> ½ cup Bacon Grease

Cut liver into thin slices. Reheat bacon grease in frying pan and add slices of Liver. Turn each slice only once. Don't cook for long, as it gets tough. A little onion salt on top enriches flavor.

NOTE: If you want to save the liver, remember to freeze the liver raw.

Venison Liver 1

1 Venison liver, sliced about ¾" thick
melted butter or margarine
onions and bacon

Brush liver with melted butter or
margarine. Broil 2" from the heat, for about 2
min. a side, until brown outside but still red
and juicy within. Saute in a frying pan 1 min. a
side.
    If sautéd: you can add onions and bacon
to your liver. Begin with the bacon in a frying
pan. Saute slowly over moderate heat, flipping
the strips over. As soon as the bacon is done,
spread it on crumpled absorbent paper to
drain, add your idea of enough diced onions to
the frying pan and saute these until golden.
Then remove from the pan and season to taste
with salt while the liver slices are sizzling 1
min to a side. End by scattering 1/3 cup of
heated brandy over the liver and igniting.
(Flambe')

Distribute the bacon and onions evenly
over each slice of venison and pour the
remaining juices over them.

Venison Liver 2

Liver, sliced thinly
Flour
Salt & pepper
1 small onion, finely chopped
5 mushrooms, finely chopped
2 tbsp. butter
2 tbsp. peanut oil
¼ cup dry vermouth

Saute onion and mushrooms in butter &
oil mixture until tender. Cover the liver slices
in seasoned flour. Push the onion and
mushrooms to the edge of the frying pan and
add the liver slices. Saute for about 8 min. (4
minutes on a side). Just before serving, add
wine, mixing with the pan juices. Place the
liver slices on a plate and cover liver with the
mushroom & onion mixture.

Deer Tongue

    1 large deer tongue
    1 tablespoon of salt
    onion
    1 bulb of garlic
    several whole cloves of garlic

    Wash the tongue well. Place in a pan and cover with boiling water. Add onion, bulb of garlic, several whole cloves of garlic and 1 tablespoon of salt. Simmer until tender.

Pit Cooked Venison

5 or 6 lb. of boned roast
salt and pepper (any other seasonings
  you desire)

Dig a pit about 18" square and line with rocks. Build a fire in the pit and let it burn down until you're left with about 6" of red coals. Place a 5 or 6 lb. of boned roast on 2 layers of heavy-duty foil, large enough to cover roast. Season with salt and pepper and any other seasonings you desire. Fold foil over the roast, sealing edges well. Place in the pit and bank coals around it. Fill the pit with dirt and cover with a darkened piece of canvas weighted down with rocks. Leave for 5 to 6 hours. Carefully remove roast from pit and open foil. Use the juices to serve over the sliced roast.

Spice Dried Venison

1 lb Venison
3 lbs. table salt
4 tbsp. allspice
5 tbsp. black pepper

Following the membrane along the muscles as much as possible, cut venison into strips, roll each piece in a mixture of table salt, allspice and black pepper, rubbing this well into the meat, then shaking off any excess. Suspend the meat on a string or wire. The treated meat must be kept dry.

About one month is needed for it to shrink and absorb the seasoning properly. Slice thin, scrape and trim some, then soak overnight if you want to cut it in bite-size chunks.

Venison Mincemeat

2 lbs. cooked venison, minced
4 lbs. chopped tart apples
2 lbs. raisins
4 cups brown sugar
¾ lb. chopped beef suet
1 to 2 ½ can apricot nectar or fruit juice
½ tsp. cloves
1 tsp. mace
½ tsp. nutmeg
2 tsp. salt
1 ½ tsp. cinnamon

Combine all ingredients. Cook very slowly until tender, about 1 hour. Place in airtight quart or pint container to keep. Process for 60 minutes at 10 lbs.

Venison Pot Pie

3 cups leftover cooked shoulder roast,
cut into bite-sized chunks
Leftover gravy
2 carrots, sliced thinly
½ lb. mushroom caps
2 tbsp. butter
Salt & pepper
Pastry for single crust
1/8 tsp. savory

Boil carrots with salt & pepper. Saute
mushrooms in the butter. Add both to the
leftover meat and gravy. Salt and pepper to
taste. Make your favorite pastry crust, adding
the savory to the flour. Place the meat mixture
in a buttered 1 quart casserole dish. Cover with
the crust, sealing the dough to the sides. Slit
the top to allow the steam to escape. Place in a
preheated 425 oven for 15 min. or until the
crust begins to brown. Turn the oven down to
350 for another 15 min. or until the meat pie is
bubbly hot.

Venison Sausage

4 lbs. venison scrap meat
½ lb. beef suet
¼ cup smoked salt
2 tsp. salt
1 ½ tsp. ground sage
½ tsp. ground allspice
¼ tsp. cayenne

Grind the venison and the suet through the coarse blade of a meat grinder. Mix in the seasonings thoroughly and grind again through with a medium blade. Stuff into casings. Bind & tie into convenient lengths.

Drop into boiling water and cook until the sausage floats, 10 to 20 min.

Deer Sausage

    5 lbs. venison
    5 lbs. pork fat
    3 tbsp. pepper
    Pinch of sage

Grind meats and seasonings together. Stuff into casings. Bind & tie into convenient lengths. Drop into boiling water and cook until the sausage floats, 10 to 20 min.

Brine Cured Venison Roll

8 to 10 lbs. venison flank
1 medium onion, peeled & chopped
2 quarts water
1 ½ cups rock salt
¾ tsp. saltpeter

Spread out flank, sewing together if you have several small ones. Sprinkle with onion. Roll tightly and tie securely. Boil water with salt until salt is dissolved. Add saltpeter. Cool the brine. Add the meat roll and store in a stone crock or glass bowl. Put a plate on top with a weight to keep the meat immersed in the brine. Leave the meat in the brine for 2 weeks too 2 months.

Remove the meat, rinse with fresh water, and boil in water. Cover & simmer for 2 hrs. Then remove from the liquid and place in a loaf pan. Put a weight on top to press it into a firm roll. Cut into thin slices, or dice and serve it cold. Can also be served in a salad.

Venison Chips

Venison, sliced ½" thick
Sourdough bread
¼ stick of butter or margarine

Melt 1/4 stick of butter or margarine in a sizzling hot fry pan. Using a spatula, lay in the 4 slices and sear 15 seconds on one side. Then add salt and pepper to taste. Tip the contents of the pan onto a hot platter. Place meat between two slices of bread for each piece.

Fried Deer Brain

1 deer brain
1 cup flour
½ cup corn oil for deep fry - (substitute
    with vegetable oil in frying pan)
Salt & pepper
Dash of cayenne & / or Cajun Season

Remove the membrane that covers the brain. Place salt, black pepper, cayenne, and flour in bowl. Gently put brain in mixture to coat entire outer area. Drop in very hot oil and fry approximately five minutes. If a large brain, it will take five minutes. If a small brain, cook until golden brown.

Baked Deer Brain

1 deer brain
½ cup flour
2/3 cup butter
½ lemon
Chopped parsley
Salt and pepper

Preheat oven to 350° F. Cut the brain in half length-wise and dip it into the mixture of flour, salt, and pepper. In a hot saucepan melt ¼ cup of butter. When the butter stops sizzling, brown the two parts of the brain. Coat regularly with remaining butter.

Cook in the oven at 350° for about 5 minutes.

www.ArdentWriter.com

CPSIA information can be obtained
at www.ICGtesting.com
Printed in the USA
LVOW10*1601060717
540467LV00011B/319/P

9 780692 768525